The Day After I Drowned

Also by Betty Bonham Lies

The Blue Laws (poetry)

The Poet's Pen: Writing Poetry with Middle and High School Students

Earth's Daughters: Stories of Women in Classical Mythology

My Ticket to Tomorrow: Activities to Explore the Past, Present, and Future

Gallery Tales: Classical Mythology in the Art Museum, Princeton University

The Day After I Drowned

Poems

Betty Bonham Lies

Cherry Grove Collections

Published by Cherry Grove Collections
P.O. Box 541106
Cincinnati, OH 45254-1106

ISBN: 9781936370092
LCCN: 2010936908

Poetry Editor: Kevin Walzer
Business Editor: Lori Jareo

Visit us on the web at www.cherry-grove.com

Grateful acknowledgement to the publications in which many of these poems first appeared:

The Comstock Review: "Sudden Appearances, the silence after" (from "Rehearsing Hell").
Cool Women, Volume 1: "The First Time," "I Wanted."
Cool Women, Volume 2: "Suppose one morning," "The Bronte Game," "Strawberry Ripe."
Cool Women, Volume 3: "I've always loved," "The Long Heart of October."
Cool Women, Volume 4: "Nothing," "The Ground That Night," "Grace," "Still Life," "Split Open."
Cool Women CD: "Cento of the Lovers."
The Edison Literary Review: "Sometimes in Your Sleep," "That's Mine."
Eye: "This Old Man."
Footsteps: "August Night."
The Journal of New Jersey Poets: "The Day After I Drowned," "Jewelweed."
Kalliope: "Rejection."
The Kelsey Review: "Bogeyman."
The Southern Review: "Tourists in Cefalù."
Mischief, Caprice, and Other Strategies: "Viva."
U. S. 1 Worksheets: "A Frontier I Never Crossed," "April Snowstorm," "Around the gods you must concentrate," "Balloonflowers," "Haunted," "Denial is a Comfortable Place."

I am grateful to many people who have helped make this book possible, especially:

Penelope Scambly Schott, who put it all together, and Lois Marie Harrod, who worked closely with me on both of my poetry books;

Cool Women poets and U.S. 1 Poet's Collaborative, for critiques;

Lynn Powell, who made me a poet again after a long hiatus;

Baron Wormser for his help and encouragement over many years; Naomi Shihab Nye, Jean Valentine, Martha Rhodes, and Vijay Sashedri;

The Geraldine R. Dodge Foundation for its support and promotion of poetry.

Contents

III. Dragonfly

I. The Bronte Game

The First Time

The first bad thing I did with a boy
was down by the kitchen door,
with Tommy Wallen.
Dark smell of earth
beneath the steps where
we sat close, tasting a word
we rolled around our mouths,
mysterious but pungent, satisfying:

> *dog shit*
> *cow shit*
> *lion shit*
> *monkey shit*

Tommy was old, my sister's age,
but he chose me instead of her,
I was always doing things she'd never
dream of, as Miss Heath
was fond of pointing out, he knew
which one of us would do it.

The day before, in that dank place
I'd stumbled over death in a wood box,
my dog's eyes crusted, gold hair dulled,
her mouth still open in a yelp of pain.

It seems like hours we lingered there,
Tommy and I, the hot word
moving in a long caress
from mouth to mouth:

giraffe shit
rhinoceros shit

suppose one morning

suppose one morning
as we dressed for work, I said
you are only life,
would you take my voice in your mouth
like a grape,
like clear water?

or if you said a truth
that fell through surface
like a flint
scraping the currents as they slide to deep,
would it turn desert back to sea?

suppose a woman ran,
her head on fire, from the sand
out of a scouring wind,
a man rose from the sea
raising his arms above him,
and we said help us, talk to us,

could we take water, sand,
and build a tower so straight
it needed no translation?

what if I said
our children are dying
or if you said I am afraid
and told your fear,

or if one night, over the last of the wine,
I leaned across the table, said
I cannot reconcile myself to death
and cried, naming your mother
and you cried for your grandmother, what then?
would it be a bandage
or a knife?

my words gather rain,
they flock on the window like moths
drinking the color of night—
will you swallow them and fill
your body full of sentence,
will they satisfy your thirst?

and if you turned to me and said
there's nothing I can't take
except your death
would it be light
rising through a pool of green water?
would it be a burning tree?

For the Dark

Lately I've thought it would be good
to cut a coat of darkness, out of whole cloth
of shadow, proof even against the flood
of moon pouring its white stone path.

If my hand could cover the sky
I'd cancel glitter from the world:
no stars, no rockets, grinning liars,
charmers, sparks that spit and turn

against the fire where they rise.
I've been years on the road to calm,
have gone through Hopewell, Hazard, Paradise,
somehow evaded the lanes of flame—

(in the town they call New Hope
stones run like honey in the sun, rivers glow
blue glass, and daytime creatures flap,
pinned by their own long shadow).

Last night I dreamed ten shady roads
but found myself once more
under the sun's thumb, that hot goad
herding me back into the glare.

It Doesn't Sleep

It calls itself man-spearer,
tiger-snarer, crowned-with-fire

thorn-eared sound-catcher.
Ah, you know it

from each empty waking,
know that soft *pad-pad*

and if a purr
breaks sudden in your ear

jump, for god's sake
jump

or breathe a prayer.

Cento of Longing

Listen: I dreamed
how it would happen—
at the edge of the light
watching stars pass
across astonishments of sky.

It's difficult to say
precisely where what had begun
to feel like reverence
becomes a sort of mournful
cosmic last resort:

in the white grass
the smooth ripple
of the wind's last name
is blood, the violet light
on a blade, a meteor.

Nothing seems different,
salt still spills upon my grave.
I glide into my cave of phantoms
all skin and bone, all woman,
unripe and raw. Tonight,

longing takes the trees.
What remains to be done?
Beyond desire there is only
more desire. Climbing the dark
I hear you coming.

Field and Sky

The time I dreamed
we weren't really married
everything seemed so easy.
It was that kind of summer day
when every leaf's a little kite
against a swoop of blue.
Our arms made fields
in which the other grew,
an always waxing moon.

Ever since that dream
I've lived whole days
thinking it's true, that
no one ever muttered words
to make us man and wife, days
when it seems we're only playing
wifman, manwo, woband
for the fun of it, no legal papers
dully signed and witnessed.

If we weren't married
and you came to my door
I'd gather you like grain,
I'd take you in so deep
that witnesses would say
how odd, at first
I thought I saw two people!
No eclipse: we'd grow together,
merge, without the trace
of a penumbra.

I am ok

I promised you; I said *I'll be ok.*
You smiled at me, your slow sweet smile.
I have been faithful to you always,

so I have to be ok, I owe it to that smile,
that gentle voice, to what we've been, together,
and when people ask me how I am, I answer,

Oh, I am ok, and I am, really am, ok
though sometimes, echoes tremble in my head:
I am ok, I am ok, I am ok,
amok.

This Old Man

When he spreads ketchup
on his long johns

she says are you sure
you want to do that

but he knows
that's how it is in spring:

your spirit spins
as if possessed

a china doll
riding a blue wild horse:

he knows there will be sun
igniting daffodils

and thunderstorms
to quench the moon:

and he salutes
the bittersweet

of time:
and when he's

good and ready
he plays One.

The Bronte Game

She is ten, and older;
she gets Charlotte. I want Emily,
the unrestrained.
We know I'll find death young
and she will marry
our father's curate, die of pregnancy.

Right now we can ignore
all that. We're still
running wild in Haworth,
turning into authors,
writing the books
we haven't read yet.

In our long skirts and hats,
discreetly veiled, we sit
at the old steamer trunk, scribbling
with feathers scattered on the lawn
by pigeons our neighbor tried to shoot
one morning very early.

We put on suits, of course,
to visit publishers.
I twirl my dark mustache:
Currer, give him the manuscripts.
She chews on her cigar. *Ellis,*
she says, *you sure know how to spin a story!*

She will be Jane, the confident,
stalwart for good;
I will be Cathy,

willful but afraid,
writing desire
against the wuthering air.

August Night

A girl slips naked from her bedroom window
to sit on the slanting porch roof just below.
From somewhere deep she feels

the day's stored heat rise into her,
she hardly hears the shrill whine
of mosquitoes discovering her flesh.

She wants to think about a kiss—
not her first,
but the first to trouble her.

She listens inward: just the swish
of blood, her metronomic heart.
She could have gone into that kiss,

down and down . . . In the yard,
the dog sets up an irritating bark.
Shut up, Cookie! Shut up!

But it's gone. Out by the barn
an owl calls, answered
by another farther off.

My Father's Lady

She'd dance herself into a lather
even before he mounted her,
his hand on her neck was enough

to stamp the pact they'd make together—
that nothing would stop them, nothing
could stand in their way, not fences,

not caution nor sense, not people—
and oh, the ride she'd take him on,
flat-out along the moonlit road

where the fields spread back dark and wide
and pungent with ripening corn, no sound
but the pound of their rhythm, their

breathing together, together they'd dare,
run up at danger and sneer it down,
run up at anyone caught in their path,

but his word in her ear, his hands
strong at her mouth, and they'd stop
like a whip, at their will, just a step

from the ending of everything,
and looking down, they'd laugh together,
stand there together, triumphant, trembling,

leaning in to become each other,
and all the world could fly to hell
for all they cared. About anything.

A Frontier I Never Crossed

Up way too high on Cracker Jack, my uncle's palomino, I was the tipside of the cliff about to fall down into Patagonia, the Andes' sharp, rainforest under cloud. Horse love, horse lover, lover of twitch and leather, sweat smell, thigh feel, lover of turning ears, I longed for you. You sitting topside in the sun, up there on Silver Lady, lady of needle nerve, loving the rush of air along your ears, loving her with your voice, murmurs of voice-line drawn so taut between you that you two were one, rider and ridden, in a country of your own. *Give a man a horse he can ride,* you sang and the song was you and the song was her and I never got inside.

Viva

The past is a book of empty pages,
nobody ever really lived in it.
Try to imagine Verdi and his Giuseppina
at their mustard-yellow villa in Busseto,
lying dark, sated with sex,
sniffing the strange perfume
coming off each other's music,
townspeople scribbling *Viva Verdi*
on the walls, or Shakespeare
about to brush the dust of Stratford off his jerkin,
screwing Anne in the next-best bed
as toads and bugs *thunk* from the thatch,
downstairs the old folks nodding
around the ingle.
     Picture your parents
licking chocolate off each other, or
heaven forbid, your mother's fragrant sigh
as you start waiting in the wings
to make your entrance
on the stage of instantly-the-past.
You'll play a short love scene,
recite some lines, forget the rest, go off.
When did the moon get full again,
spilling its cup of borrowed light
as if that petty glare could clarify,
illuminate, convince you anything
was ever real?
     None of it happened,
all of it is happening, it's done with mirrors,
strings of them, wavy and fogged,
reflecting everything at once,

the nothing that is there.
And even as you're writing new scripts
with the sharp pencil of *now*
a big white gum eraser follows close behind
and the moon struts its pocky show
against the seamy backdrop of black space.

Leave-Taking

My window opens on a lane of light.
I'll carve your name against the moon's fine shell,

let sorrow be beginning, just another road to follow
when the dark notes call, when wind blooms white

over the Sourland hills. *Departure* could mean *peace,*
leave be the name of blossoming.

I've Always Loved

I've always loved
the men who must be wooed,

the king who didn't have to talk:
riding under a small-grained moon,

all colors of the snowy road
curved in to fit his waist,

the Horse King with three eyes:
he called me Rose. Little Swallow.

Iris. Ash. The Least One.
In his mouth I knew the name was mine.

Asleep under a quilt of tulip petals
feathered like the wings of birds,

the grain of something imperceptible
gashed the instep of my foot,

to this day I wear the scar,
although I never point to it.

A small room hung with carpets,
swirl of leaves left in the cup,

my future was laid out
—mirrors, shreds of fabric,

the king of iron water:
he told me I was salable,

foot washing, towel, basin.
I longed to run away.

Two times I've drowned,
I know the undertow,

the loss of vertical,
head hitting bottom.

Perhaps my instinct
was the right one after all:

I had already drowned
and who could say I wouldn't drown again

looking for the king
of hell-for-leather,

foaming and stamping in his stall,
too hot for me to handle.

II. The Long Heart of October

Mixing Metaphors

You burst on my life
like a tongueful of cloves
and rattled all the bottles
on my spice rack.
My heart drew still
as the heart of a whirlwind.

We chose to paddle
a double kayak,
set up our reactions
under a single hood:
they can be flinty, wind-torn
like the Faulkland Islands,
or strange and jade
as an Amazonian rain forest.

Sometimes we compose in a minor key,
but always resolve to the major.
My love keeps rising
like a sun-struck barometer,
till now, my exponential love,
I love you to the forty-sixth.

Complaint of the Well-Mannered Poet

Don't think I do not feel
because I do not tell you
that I feel

My life, it's true
(so far) has lacked
impacted tragedy

but things have happened
to me too
that if I told

would make you sad
and much worse things are pending
as we speak

But I was more than taught
to be upbeat
(no matter what)

It was the very heart
of family
you might assert

It is our ethos
rather, manners:
it is not polite to say

that anything is wrong
and we avoid all that
by keeping busy

happy being busy
happiest when we are
busiest

Buzz buzz

But as a poet
I'm supposed
to lay my sadness out

for you to know
my courage:
Oh the poems

I might give you
but for manners,
manners!

Bogeyman

In the Black Hills, when I was small,
there were two bogeymen. The one
outside, snuffling around the window
high above our iron cots, even then
I guessed to be my oldest cousin, Tom.
The other had no name to tame it by,

only Aunt Marguerite at dusk
beside the stream, bending over fire
to fry up frogs' legs
in a black iron skillet, where
they jumped and skipped as if
they might be trying to escape.

Grandpa, in one smooth gesture, slung
a chicken on the chopping block—*ka-whunk!*—
flung it aside to reel about the yard.
Its ruffled neck threw out long strings of blood
until it toppled in the dusty grass
where it began to lose its sheen.

Today I picked nine roses, lustrous still
after last night's hard frost. At the market,
everyone was running up and down the aisles
knocking into other shoppers. It's always
like that now. It may be we're all dead,
just haven't caught on yet.

April Snowstorm

Look at my jonquils
buried under snow:

last week I dreamed this storm,
today it came.

I dreamed I knew death,
how it smells

like fungus
crawling fallen logs

like liver frying
in the blackened pan.

They said you only
have to taste it

taste a tiny piece,
it's good for you

they said
it's good for you

like touching
your grandmother's skin

so wax and chill
so almost buried

yellow, white
so jonquil-under-snow.

Even the Polestar Drifts

Wading marsh shallows drowned with rain
I hardly can remember waking with him late

to a white world, straight alleys of stone,
the clear water of truth-telling. Here,

shreds of bone spell out a name unasked-for
like a fortune teller's patchwork remedy.

I should have asked:

did something happen in some other century
that could explain my wanders?

Even a nameless stream is a frightening thing

(Buson)

Everyone knows what happens
in a wood: you lose yourself,
circle eternally
the same trees with their slide of moss
and knowing moss grows
only on the north won't help

because you haven't any notion
what direction out lies anyway
and nothing has a name—
the bear, the wolf, the tree,
this stream you've crossed before—

you touch some greenish stuff
crawling up one side of
tall rough things
that raise their arms to sky,

and wonder what you're doing here
but can't imagine
what *here* means.

The Day After I Drowned

The day after I drowned
I got up, dressed, and went to school.
Nothing was different: nobody saw me

on the bus, or greeted me
when I got off, no wave and shout
to save a seat for them at lunch.

I found an empty desk and sat
as still as water. Teacher
didn't see me there, or not,

even the teasers haven't noticed.
Nothing is different. But every day
I come and go,

I come and go
and I watch all of you,
remembering the scratch of sand

scrubbing my forehead,
bubbles rising bright
as your birthday balloons,

the surface far up overhead
like a moon so white
that for a flash I understood

the black that lies beyond.
You don't see me, but
if you take a picture of this room

I'll be there somewhere
in the negative.

Sometimes in your sleep

you sigh and slip into a silence empty as a breath,
and then I know you've gone into the room

that lies so far from me I cannot even guess
what colors light its walls, what shadows crawl

across the floor. Your absence spreads
along the headboard of the bed where we lie

side by side, as if we equally inhabited this life
we've shared for forty years. But each of us

lives in a different place, our front rooms always
open to the other, sometimes darker spaces—

Those long hallways, doors beyond doors,
the last one opening upon . . . .

Some things frighten me, a box
from which plagues have escaped,

a stone pushed back to show a vacant tomb,
a house without you in it.

Tourists In Cefalù

Below the looming skull of stone, sea breaks,
three shades of blue, and we've been dazed

by a cathedral's dome, that gold mosaic
Christ, so cool, inclusive, arms embracing all

of Sicily's invaders, with his blond Norman hair
and Arabic black beard, his Byzantine long nose.

Back in the square, under a broad umbrella,
we sip our dark espresso. A sudden motion:

crowns and crowns of funeral flowers
rivaling the sun, and then a coffin

carried in procession from the church. The priest
in black, a line of mourners: widow walking, bent,

the family weeping; at the rear, joking and gossip.
You rise as they pass by our table: your eyes

brighten with tears, and I am thinking
that my single indrawn breath diminishes

what breath is left to me, but you are thinking
of the man himself, nailed in a box, never

to sweat under the sun, to feel again
his knuckles scraping rock, the salt sting

at his hands as he hauls in the net,
silver with leaping fish.

Time Change

A rosy yellow glow
hangs in the air for hours tonight:
I want to go outside with you
to sit once more on the front steps and smoke
while from their cribs the children,
calling like young doves,
complain of being put to bed
in such a long twilight

and insects start the spring's thin hum,
forsythia flare rockets of bright gold,
magnolias lift pale cups of bloom
to a slowly changing sky:
our cigarette ends flash and dart
like the fireflies soon to come
as we rough out illimitable futures
until dark paints over the last lines of light

and finally it's decent
to go in to bed.

The Long Heart of October

This year's fall has been like sex, the best sex,
like the sex your mother didn't tell about, or if she did
you didn't listen, mortified that she could say such things,

could know about the sweet slow building
to the brink, each day glowing deeper till you ache
with longing never to arrive, but keep on coming.

My mother has been old for thirty years,
dropping her leaves gently one by one. I meet her
at the entrance to the forest, say her name over

like a lover. *Mother.* Tell me what I need to know:
what I should watch for, watch out for. This time
I swear I won't be so embarrassed I can't hear you.

Jewelweed

We call it *touch-me-not,* this wildness
tense as a spring: *Hands off,*
it seems to say, but I know
something wound up
in the heart's green coils
is crying *Touch me. Touch me.*
Touch me now. All fall
I have been drawn and drawn again
to one tall stand of jewelweed,
to touch the pendant seedpods,
feel them burst with life.
I understand it's not just botany
that gives me such delight
running my fingers over their plumpness,
warming them till they explode
and scatter seed.
I have seen hummingbirds
bury their beaks in jeweled cups,
the bees delving so deep
you only know they're inside
by the flower's orange tremblings.
This autumn, when my body
keeps its secrets from me,
hiding something deep within,
it pleases me to feel
the life stored in those pods,
waiting for release, first now,
and then again to rise,
to rise after a slow cold winter.

Haunted

now when our nights
are webbed with shadows

of the future   I wake again
dream-wondering

what was that tapping
on my shoulder

tolling over in my head

and then I know

it's you

you on my tongue
like licorice

and the dark of your breath
in my ear

stay I whisper *stay*
but even as I'm saying it

I feel you slide away

Rejection

What if your lover said I'm sorry,
you don't meet my current needs,
smiling kindly across the breakfast table
as he salts his egg (over easy, just
the way he likes it),
I've gone over your work carefully, he adds,
buttering an English muffin, and while
it's strong, it isn't what I'm looking for
right now. One effort—no, two—came close,
he goes on as he spreads the honey,
thank you for letting me consider it.
He gulps his coffee. This does not necessarily imply
a criticism of your merit. I hope,
as he puts on his coat, you will try again.
One quick kiss and he's out the door.
The words float back, I wish you best of luck
in placing yourself elsewhere.

Sudden Appearances

The slither of your dry palm over mine
makes secret rustles like a snake

passing through last year's leaves—
I don't know where it came from,

where it's going. I startle easily:
a love sign, snake, or finding,

out among my roses, casual gift:
a whole and perfect skin, dying to show

its mysteries to the finder, wild design,
even the eyes were covered by a shuff of skin.

Between our fingers, spaces like the cool holes
in a wall of rocks, and something hiding there.

Strawberry Ripe

They ripen on their way to market,
so when I was a girl I was taught to pick
too soon, to pluck them pink
as my virgin nipples, and as firm,

but now I've schooled myself to wait
until they're ready, bursting red—

Is anything this red? I mean
this perfect early-season-ripening red,
this lush and rich too deep for finger-cut-blood red,
for end-of-summer-setting-sun red,
red of roses, even fully blown.

It's summer's warming sign, this red,
strawberry red, this incubating red
like inner blood, like woman's blood,
this fertile red, this promissory red—

till now all of creation spreads around me
like a treasure trove, seducing me to search
beneath its canopy of green and find out riches,
sweet and red and ripe, and fill my bowl,
and fill my greedy mouth.

Cento of the Lovers

Between the peony and the rose
there is a field, so secret
that the very sky seems small.

Nights under a pale moon
and geraniums, vast orange dreams
are unclenched: look how he leans into her

to talk of unfamiliar things in a low familiar voice.
Look how she glances down the evening,
lighting the candles one by one,

the cold splintering, breaking slow
out of the darkness,
each night bonded to the next.

The wet fern of her hair,
the smell of braids, wind plaited
in the mouth of the loved one,

and the world is changed as if
two people shaken by dizziness and enlaced
are fallen among the grass:

And they are, they are,
the wind and the mountains and the half moon
lift them up, bright in the pure, black air,

their bodies luminous. The little
sucked-in breath, tremors along the skin,
say the words *yes,* and *good,* and mean them.

At the edge of the light there is a field.
Treetops, prolific as the sky, drift in lacy jags.
To him, that place is real, and is forgiving;

to her, a circle of light, holy ground.
In the spring rain
the birds fall silent in the woods.

Nothing remains the same

In the dry time before the river
rose to flood my dreams

I lay down drowsy as a woodchuck,
hid unlistening,

the spindle of the wind
wound a fine web around me.

Safe in the shade I wouldn't hear
the widening wings, the lightning,

and my mouth a moth
folding its green transparency

denying everything.

Nothing

Nothing about the food, the wine,
the talk, could tell why everything
went wrong: it was the best
of restaurants, the oysters icy,
tanging of the sea, lamb pink
and sweet inside its seasoned crust,
wine tendering our tongues
strengthened our tongues enough
to speak the truth. We talked of
things that mattered: art and poetry,
the past, and love. When did we start
to feel uneasy, start to drop our eyes
and find words faltering? What pushed itself
into our moment, circling unheard,
laying its chill along our skins
till even breath came hard? That uninvited third,
that thing unspeakable we do not
wish to know—not long ago unthinkable,
it's always breathing at us now.

Denial is a Comfortable Place

In this new place
against the odds

I'm cooking my heart out
for you: sirloin with bearnaise sauce,
cheesy potatoes, chili, ravioli, quiche,

even a chocolate pie—all that good stuff
we gave up years ago. I'm playing
we are anywhere but where we are:

a Hamburg evening, suckling pig and artichokes,
slow walks along the Alster, and at dusk
a long necklace of light all down the Elbe:

or the Camargue, flamingo feathers rosy,
furling on wind against the ramparts
of a stony tower, fish soup with aioli, duck breast, rare:

camped at Green River, rainbow trout
smoked on our fire, our tent flaps open
to the beavers' path, sleeping sweetly hip to hip:

lobster and corn and candles on the porch
dark in a thunderstorm while a child flits,
a small white moth, intoning kum-by-ya:

In this new place
against the odds

all day I'm hiding from the dragon
of the waterfall Catastrophe. All night
he finds me, whispers: No, it's true. It's true.

Split Open

Doesn't it feel sometimes as if
your life's that yellow Shop-Rite bag
the cashier packed so carelessly, so fast,
and when you're in the steaming parking lot
it splits and spills out all the things
you chose so carefully:

an orange rolls under that obese SUV
nobody should be driving anyway,
tomatoes hit ground with a *thup!* the eggs
splat open, and then there you are, down
on your knees in new white pants
scrambling to pick up dirty lettuce,
bruised pears, wandering apples,

but of course, you have no bag
to put them in, nobody stops to offer help,
you're on your own now, trying not to cry,
trying to make the best of it, this situation
you are not to blame for, but you're stuck there,
deal with it. It's not the worst. You know already
there's a ten-ton truck heading your way,
careening around the corner of tomorrow.

III. Dragonfly

In the hospital where you lost your voice

where everything went haywire,
the hospital that turned into a prison,
where you lost your shell-shaped voice,
where I tried to translate your lips' slow moving
after you couldn't tell your story any more,

in the prison where they cut holes in your
stomach, in your throat, where your cheeks
hollowed into caves, where your spine
stood up like a mountain ridge,

in that hospital where nurses
didn't look at you as they poured liquid
in your feeding tube, where doctors
thought a shoulder touch denoted
sympathy, in that prison where

summer felt like steel in winter,
where fear commanded all my thinking,
in that grey hospital where your
melodious tenor voice was stilled,
we didn't need an oracle to hint
the story of our future.

And now I dial our number just to hear
your voice on the machine say once again,
Sorry, I can't talk with you just now.

Rehearsing Hell

1. Diagnosis

The wolves' trail leads away
beyond a lake of waters
black as raven thought.

Panic is leaping from the trees
with shoulders hunched:
it breathes at me and cries.

A white rock drops.
I too am sinking,
pocketing my stones of love

as the moon turns its face away
and will not speak.

2. Waiting Room

The fortune-teller grins,
clenching our future
in hard gnarly hands, her crystal
feathery with smoke. Joan Rivers brays,
her face so tight her eyes are almost
in her ears, then three cats harmonize
with *meow meow meow meow.* Regis

arrives by cab, snapping the ice-white cuffs
of his slick tux, hands out a slippy blonde
in a magenta boob-loosed gown, flaunting

a cool two mil in diamonds
on her chest. Dear God,

it's only fucking nine a.m.! I jump up
from my stiff black chair, go try another.
Hard. I know they're all the same,
but some mad hope makes me
keep changing anyway. Out of

the whiff side of my eye I catch you
going bent through a far door, clutching
your street clothes to your chest, two ass-length
flowered gowns worn back to front.
The cats *meow meow,* while Joanie shrieks,
Regis takes center stage at some award show,
everybody's screaming there and it is
fever pitch in this room too.

We eye each other slantwise, feet and hands
in twitchy motion, wondering whose name
will surface next. Uneasy, we begin to test
our chance companions: *when was yours
supposed to go? When did you see him last?* The
diamond-splattered wallpaper is
closing on me. Air! The cats

meow meow, Regis has just been given
an award. Outrageous. You
have disappeared behind those wide-slung
automatic doors, into the ravined maw of
modern medicine, some place
I'm not allowed to see. Cats *meow,*
Joan barks. Regis peacocks. I've lost

all track of time and everything I
used to think I knew. This day's strung
like the beads of Hell. I haven't even
hit the bad stuff yet.

3. the silence after

a bite-sized night
the moon's too full to enter

and beyond the river sits
the wolf with human eyes

something's knocking
ardent at the door

but when I open no one's
out there   only me

barefoot in this place
breathing the wind

a dead tree bursts
like pollen in my hands

and just beneath the leaf
a planetary dust

now every stone sings
nothing without end

Waiting for you to die: a cento

I might accept anything:
the stars at daybreak
where two worlds touch,
wild hair in the wind
and haze and vista. . .

Through our guessing silence
you tell me of our future,
how I might survive,
a star among stars,
a melting of green waters.

I want to believe
but I am in flight
across the night sky.
Outside it is still cold.
The window grows slowly dark.

I am not dead.
I watch myself in the glass
walking barefoot at the start of spring
after the vanished harvest.
What is it going to be like

along that road, remembering
the bright unbroken planet
of our love
spilling like smoke
into the morning dust?

Elevator Number Two in Rahway Hospital

I thought the arrow
pointed *up*

but when I stepped in
an alarm screeched

no, too fast! too fast!
and we went into

free fall and that's all
I can remember

till we hit the bottom

and yes, you're dead,
I'm dead,

we're all dead,
still,

surprisingly
we try and try

to find
some back way up.

Simple Things

Soffits are the subject
of their conversation; son and husband
understand you need to keep them dry.

How do men know the things
they know? I'm sure
in my son's growing up
they never spent an hour together
over soffits.

If you're responsible for something,
then you learn, they answer me.

My husband has been teaching me
some things I'm going to have to know
before too long: simple things now,
like how to play a DVD, replace
the light bulbs in the ceiling fixtures,
run the snowblower, spray for weeds.

Too soon it will be harder tasks,
helping him dress, turning him over
in his bed, letting him choose
if he prefers to use a respirator
or to die.

Last night I dreamed I was a man,
naked in the moonlight, struggling
to put on my jockey shorts.

Dragonfly

I saw it yesterday
hover above our house

when you weren't here.
I didn't hear it coming,

sharp grey needle, wings
that cast no shadow.

Air went stiff,
I couldn't take a breath.

Your absence hung
like stone: I tried to

cup it in my hand
to throw it far away.

And then the dragonfly,
its black transparency.

I wouldn't wait if I were you

You will need patience
if you want to see me cry
because I'm stone

and water doesn't rise from stone
but only washes over it

and it takes centuries
to wear stone down
to start to carve

the red rimmed lids
between which water runs

millenia to knife down deeper
canyoning stark walls
down eons of existence

and by then it's gone so deep
that even from your high lookout

you'll barely see the flow
now bending gently through the cut
its violence once worked

exposing first rock of the world

Vishnu
       Preserver
              Husband

After All

It wasn't death that was our enemy,
we'd learned to live with him.

All summer there was dying,
little dyings: grass, the roses,

your car first, then my car,
mower, washer. . . no, it wasn't death,

it was the waiting, anxious,
like waiting for the toaster,

or the other shoe, the last
note of the scale:

all tension, expectation,

as if we somehow needed it
for our completion,

and it seemed right
that everything we had

was going first,
was showing us the way.

The Ground That Night

The ground that night lay heavy
as if death weighted
every step along the way

I moved by indirection
and the trees hissed rain
rain deafened me

my mother's voice inside
my head felt holy
like a text I couldn't read

but had to learn by heart:
the book of contradictions

Midweek

Wasn't it bad enough that Tuesday
they stopped me outside your door
while green-clad men clustered around your bed

and I was herded to another room
and told it was time to "let you go?"

Wednesday was worse. Wednesday I had to choose
which of your meds to stop.
You burned with fever.

Thursday you rallied, you seemed better,
and I came to worst:

Thursday I was afraid you wouldn't die.

Reading a Death Certificate

Do not abbreviate. Enter
only one cause per line.
Add additional lines if necessary.

Do not enter terminal events
such as cardiac arrest
or ventricular fibrillation
without showing etiology.

Do not abbreviate.

I get all that.
But what to make of his death
in that sloppy doctor's hand:
Venterntor depemonfntt relpiahtumy cacunk

Somebody, please,
just make it clear:
Why did he die?

Do not abbreviate.

What the Fortune Cookie Said

Something good will arrive by mail
when you are least expecting it—
a jewel, a map, two rings of gold,
a letter from someone you have lost.

When you are least expecting it,
something you thought could never come true:
a letter from someone you have lost,
like a bell tolling the *Ode to Joy*,

something you thought could never come true.
And your heart will swell and start to sing
like a bell tolling the Ode to Joy
beyond the limits of earth and sky.

Your heart will swell and start to sing
a tune that soars above things of this world:
beyond the limits of earth and sky,
you'll start to live in your life again.

Your tune will soar above things of this world—
a jewel, a map, two rings of gold.
You might start to live in your life again
if something good did arrive by mail.

Everyone Says I'm Doing Well

The last week of your life I held your hand
through the prison bars on your hard bed,
too high to reach you with my kiss.

We didn't talk much. How could we
tell each other what we knew?
You asked me—voice straining against

the respirator—*What's the point?*
All I could answer was, *I think you've done
your time in Purgatory now.*

Outside the windows of your room,
the ash trees swayed in endless,
pointless, movement. No one had ever

taught me what to do with this,
there was no college course called
Death of Husband 101. Some cultures know

how to give tongue to grief.
I wish I did. How do those women
make that sound, that flexing cry?

How do they use their tongues to shriek
what is unspeakable, unthinkable,
and true?

The first dream

is the dream of greed, abundance warm and wet and soft, so
plentiful it almost smothers you. Baskets of candy underneath
the bridge, uncounted unnamed treasure, glittering.

Next is the dream of fear, the witch moves in next door, steals
all your plenty, that thing chasing you has half a face, your
feet are welded to the ground. Tornadoes roar, black as the
world. You fall.

The dream of failure, you stand up before your class wearing
a flannel nightgown and you've never read the book, don't
know the students, then you see the school board lined up in
the back, their eyes avid on you.

The dream of hope.

The dream of colors, a low yellow house, the jade-green lake
that lights your face as you cross in your cobalt boat beneath
star-salted midnight sky.

The dream of dailiness, you wake to the alarm, shower and
dress, eat breakfast, leave for school, go through the first two
classes, then the alarm goes off, you wake, shower and dress...

The dream of sex, Sean Connery/James Bond and you outwit
the spies, keep giddy balance as you run along the ridge pole,
and it all ends right, just you and James, just you.

The dream of tenderness.

The dream of loneliness, out on a naked road, you walk
a crimson field littered with alabaster statues, perfect
noiselessness.

The dream of loss, your child was kidnapped, tortured, your
grandchild run down by a truck: why did you put her bed out
on the road?

The dream of being lost, you can't find home, you come down
off a scaffold to an unfamiliar lake, the tunnel has no end.
What is the way? Now lives depend on you, room after room
is added to the old brick school you have to scurry through,
you're running out of time.

The dream of death.

Some Kind of Wedding

The beach this morning: bridal waves,
their wind-borne veils—
a storm too far away to see
drove them to shore.
Black clouds marched down
the clear aisles of the sky.

I never wanted every girl's dream wedding,
costly white dress, two hundred guests,
bouquet of stephanotis, only wanted
you and me saying *we love,*
saying *forever,* wanted not to see
the smear of distant clouds
lined up in dark procession.

I think I always guessed
perfection is illusion;

still I dream these dreams: in our garage
we hug, I feel the hard knot of your back,
inhale your ironed shirt. So I pretend
there's something constant, that
some way we're still together
out beyond the what I know:

the sea   the waves   the clouds
the wind

I Don't Want Much

I only want you back.
Or just to hear your voice.
I'd like its tender tones, soft sibilance,
the beauty of its timbre, but I'd take it
mad, I'd even take it mad at me. I want
your hands, making and fixing,
holding the newspaper. I want them
easy on the steering wheel. I want them
touching me. I want you sitting in your chair
listening to Mahler, with a book, or you
just sitting there and thinking. I want you
mowing the lawn. I want you with me
on the plane going to China.

Damn this new life.
I want our conversations. All these months
I've sat alone at dinner with a book. Music
and candlelight don't give me company.

I want you back.

Humours

I used to take comfort
in dry things: stone
and glass and steel,
eddies of brown oak leaves
outside my door, ash,
bone.

Now I desire long rain
to scour my window,
somebody's breathing
moist against my cheek,
a sea riding beneath me
when I fall.

Grace

An elbow bends tender as fern.
Ribs arch to a cathedral's groin,
flex like the bow of yew
a hunter draws.

Skin sings its flute notes
even at a graveside and denies
the tyranny of death.

My mouth remembers
how one pomegranate seed
could slip free of the fruit,
my tongue a dancer
in the honey flesh.

I catch a whiff of some tomorrow
in your eyebrow's arch, narrow
and perilous. Our bridge
is glass: walk over softly,
lest it shatter.

I wrap your life around me
like a millefleur shawl.
I want to live inside you, larval
in my chrysalis, suspended,
safe, until I have to move out
from the shell.

An empty cup has its own grace
if it was first well made.

IV. Balloonflowers

Still Life

A white horse. Wings. And the dead.
Sleet silvering the yellow leaves of fall.

You sit in your chair, hands folded,
gathering dust. Graying.

Unlock your eyes, your tongue.
A door is there, beyond the bricks,

a window looking out to evergreens,
a pebbled path. A table, set.

They will remain—the effigy in gold,
the stiff hard robes. But there are

snowdrops blossoming,
and friends. A pear. A chalice.

Gifts you hardly know
how you can open.

Pumas have been sighted in this Township

Some nights we used to hear
an animal we couldn't name,
a sound between a scream and groan.

In my dream, a man
stands at the back door
begging to come in.

Pawprints on my driveway
prowl about both cars,
too big to be a house cat's.

The last few nights,
my comforter hasn't been enough,
the blue comforter. Blue sheets.

Shadow of my pillow
on the wall this morning,
black and long.

This first spring warmth,
I try to blow away
last year's stubborn leaves.

Something today about the wind. . .
Something about the daffodils. . .

Cleaning a closet yesterday,
I found a bag of batteries,
labeled in his slant hand:
Not Dead.

Periodic Table

White horse on the road ahead.
White cross on the mountain.

White tulips in an old man's hand.
Earth and stone and water.

At Cedar Lake

What scared me was the man
who grabbed me up so unexpectedly
there at the drop-off,

lugged me from the water,
coughing, plunked me down
beside my mother. Not the lake—

it welcomed me, in fact, its cold
a tantalizing cap, closing delicious
on my head as I slipped down—

the green look of the water, rising
drops of air, my hair a feathery weed.
Below, such sharp clear stones; above, the sky

white, solid, like the underside of ice.
A muted world, cut off from
all that movement and the calling voices:

at once I recognized it, always knew
that this would happen. But then it didn't,
so we had our lunch.

The beach was shady, grass banks
dropping, steep. Dark trees ran down
almost to the water line. My limbs

lethargic, oddly light, I sat
clean in the pull of after swim,
hungry but somehow satisfied,

my flesh sweet, juicy as the plums
we sucked to quench our thirst,
as tangy just below the skin.

That's Mine

That's mine,
that one, that
hot-off-the-show-floor Porsche,
flashing redder than the neon
shouting *Harry's Bar and Grill*
out on route forty-one,
and when I slam into the parking lot
the guys will drop their Buds,
fog up the window, just to watch
me getting out,

I want that body, low and sleek,
want to climb out of it, so slow, my dress
riding up to here
and I don't care, I want
that new car smell, that
leather, soft upholstery,
I want to charge it up
with my perfume and
anything that comes,

I want to drive it 90 miles an hour
right through this lousy town
and feel it cut the air in two,
and blow you, baby, off your feet,
and then when you come round again
drooling at my chassis,
to beg me for a ride,
what do you think I'll do?

You think I'll give you one?

I Wanted

I wanted a wolf,
yellow-eyed and hungry.
I wanted howling,
tones strung out so thin and tense
it's like a czardas played on nerves.
I wanted thunderstorms
with winds to rock the world,
lightning bolting down like hail.
I wanted fire.

I hadn't thought of what
they might consume.
Appetite, for one. To be
well-fed is not all good,
sleekness forgets
the bite of need,
how to prowl, to leap,
grows slow and lazy.

These days when I cry
my face turns so ugly
I can't stand to see myself,
my mouth a grimace,
drooping like a mask.

What I need is yellow eyes
and hunger, hunger.

Cento of the Worm

I am almost afraid
to write down this thing:
there is a worm in the human heart,

as false as air, as water.
There is nothing more
that I can say or lose.

Did you look back?
The only place I had left to go
was some old house where we had lived.

It was terrible how quiet it was:
a syllable might lift the roof,
a mirror leap at you.

Did I not remember the curse of this place,
the chill and windwhip?
Our echoes died in that corridor.

We wanted to hold what we had,
but we were locked in with loss
like mist on the windows of dead houses.

Mountains lift. Circling the cliff-side path
along an ocean coast, I write your name,
and climb the mountain as if I were

the residue of some stranger's life.
I want to call someone
and lie: *No longing any more.*

Late Evening

Far down the street she hears
the neighbor's dog not barking

She smells her husband
making no popcorn

Feels him not touch her breast
not lick her ear

She and her heart lie beating
at a nailed-down door

Places I never kissed until it was too late

the V between
your thumb and forefinger

jut of your skull
behind the ear

your smallest toe
skin of your elbow

night-breath
soft as secret rain

the corner of your laugh
your mind-quirks

quickness
silences

the sure struts
of the span

that held me up
above the pit

Schicksalslied

Langsam und sehnsuchtsvoll (Brahms)

Down-bone
the old ones knew
what I pretend I don't:

Fate won't be kind.

I thought I'd make
an Ode to Joy,
compose harmonics

in a sunny key
to sing our lives through
to the end.

Too late I see
the reaching shadows,
swift shift to the minor.

Time flirts and passes
like a slender girl,
humming seductively.

This is the song of Fate,
the master says. *Now play it,*
slow and yearningly.

not your mother's werewolf

ghost of a memory
just out of mind

lurking around the corners
of the night:

a subcutaneous cut
that smarts but doesn't bleed

it's not your mother's werewolf

not inherited, your own

creation, woven out of
itchy 4 a.m.'s

furred with regrets
fangy with sorrows

and
familiar

Eurydice's Version

Every girl dreams about a man like that,
not handsome merely, all-around,
an athlete, stars in his own band—
the whole town's hero, might be half a god,

aloof—then, just one look at you
and he's a goner! Suddenly you've got
his letter sweater or his ring,
you stand to watch him, glowing in his light,

and everybody hangs on him,
they worship him, your dog,
your grandmother, your friends
would die to take your place.

What's more, this man adores you
to the point of madness, there is nothing
he won't do for you. He'd
go through hell for you.

And still, somehow it all ends up
his story, a tale of skill and daring,
what he did for you
and how he did it,

what he saw and what he said.
At last it hardly matters
how you came to be
among the shades,

you limp out when you're called
to take your place and track
his shadow through the dark.
Then he turns around.

This is the part your mother
never told you, noone seemed to know.
It's not all perfect,
being loved so much.

Around the gods, you must concentrate

Just for that moment
you let down your guard,
an instant of not noticing

juice dripping from the stems
of blossoms you are picking
to make a posy for your child,

juice strangely red,
the petals shuddering as if
they felt some agony, and you

can't move, you're rooting,
bark already has begun
to work its way around your legs,

and it's no good to plead
you meant no harm, your whole life
has been innocent of wrong intent:

the gods, aloof as lotus,
never listen to such cries,
no going back from this misstep,

so call the ones you love,
give them a kiss
before the wood claps shut,

before it covers up your lips,
before it closes down your eyes,
and let them feel how rough

your body's grown,
warm at first, then cooling
right beneath their hands.

Balloonflowers, November

Three white blooms still
immaculate against the blackened echinacea

open like a parachute
you could grab hold of and float up

a full moon hanging on the night
or you could choose to stay

rooted
in this world I mean

Cento of Loss

Late afternoon on the street,
a mirage, a moon of white

and the sky stacked against me:
everything was in the air,

stars burning out and falling
like seagulls in the wake of a ship.

In the long unsleeping nights
what stillness over house and garden,

my footsteps like water, hollow.
I count the holes they leave. Yes,

things have come to that.
In the terrible hours of the window,

I stand trembling,
a little mist of fallen starlight,

the dark blood in my body stunned
and unaware, not anything like sleep:

the same bewildered face of a child
who senses first responsibility,

how to stand up, knowing
we must lose what we love.

Since then it has not stopped raining,
all the flowers going inward,

cornflowers and Queen Anne's lace,
the wind, in its greatest power, whirls,

chunks of land at mid-sea disappear.
Come back! come back. . .

In the cave of my ruins,
only the candle flames.

It's never done,
this work of burial.

Morphine Pump

Miraculous machine
that lets me feed myself
if not surcease, then ease

that feels something like love—
It won't let you take too much, they say
you can't get hooked on this

but now I find myself
another kind of junkie
waiting for pain, loving the pain

the sting of blackened arms,
the broken limbs,
the stabs of breathing,

because this pain I can treat

with only seven pumps
this pain will soften
lose its bitter edge

why hasn't someone thought of
a device to make it painless
losing you?

Now

You only have to say a word
five or six times for it to lose
all meaning. Try it now:
say sorrow, sorrow, sorrow, then
tomorrow, morrow, morrow.

Today I ironed all his shirts
to give away. It seemed to hallow
them, and me, somehow, it felt as if
he just was lying fallow, that
he could be back again
to sow and grow and mow,

and now it's hard to swallow
my life's hollowness, believe
I will not follow him
into tomorrow.

Wearing the willow,
they used to call it,
but I don't know why,
because of weeping, maybe,
bending over, hair low at the neck
like someone headed for the gallows.

But I have sworn I will not
wallow in that shadow, bellow
even to my pillow,
though some narrow
early morning wakings
pow! a sneaky blow.

I have to say it now, I know, I have to
say that word, say it again,
again, until it has no force: and so
I stammer—willow   window   widow—
damn it, allow it, say it,   widow
say it again, say   widow,
widow,   widow, widow, widow.

Day Breaks

I'm way up on the roof but I'm not scared
I know the ending will be fine

then something strikes my head
my eyes scratch open   dark

dark as the gullet of a yellow dog
6:40   and I stumble

up to day   I want to stay
inside the chrysalis of dream

I'm still the unchanged worm
I try to open wings   but they clump

crumpled   wet and thick
no lift for me   no flight

the sun raises his bleary eye
glares over the reddened lid

of this day   soulless as
every other day I free fall through

no parachute
no bungee cord to bounce me back

and still too dark to see
the end

CPSIA information can be obtained at www.ICGtesting.com
Printed in the USA
269871BV00001B/43/P